I0414001

17 Prehistoric Beasts

EVERYONE SHOULD KNOW ABOUT

STANTON F. FINK

VOLUME X OF STANTON'S COLORING BOOKS

Acknowledgments

and Dedication

To my father, in whose books I discovered my first monsters.

To Will Caligan, whose help and encouragement is one of the primary reasons for this coloring book's existence.

To Mariano Silvera, who should have had his own artbooks

To Doctor David Morafka, who helped teach me to be more picky with my information.

To my friends, who helped push me to make this.

Table of Contents

Introduction

The purpose of this coloring book series is to provide information on various prehistoric animals both profoundly famous and incredibly obscure to artists of all ages. Of course, there is a lot of material to work with, as animals have been a major component of Earth's ecosystems for at least 670 million years.

For the sake of space and workability, each volume will contain 17 entries: ideally, one species for each geological time period, if possible. If you, or your inner and or outer child do not see your favorite prehistoric animal here, it may be eventually featured in another volume. Or, contact me to have it put into a later volume.

Glossary

- **Aquatic**- Living in water.
- **Arthropod**- Any member of the animal phylum Arthropoda, including trilobites, arachnids, crustaceans, insects, myriapods and their relatives. All arthropods have armor-like, jointed exoskeletons made of chitin-derived plates, sometimes reinforced with calcium carbonate, and jointed limbs.
- **Cambrian**- A period of time in the Paleozoic Era from 541 to 485 million years ago.
- **Carboniferous**- A period of time in the Paleozoic Era from 359 to 300 million years ago.
- **Cenozoic**- An era of time in the Phanerozoic Eon from 65 million years ago until now.
- **Chordate**- Any member of the animal phylum Chordata, including sea squirts, lancet fish, and vertebrates (such as lampreys, sharks, tuna, frogs, lizards, chickens, and people). All chordates have, at least at some point in their life cycle, a notochord, a long, flexible rod, usually made of cartilage, or, in the case of most vertebrates, cartilage and bone, running down the back from head to tail, directly beneath the neural tube.
- **Cnidarian**- Any member of the animal phylum Cnidaria, such as jellyfish, box jellies, Portuguese Man'o'war, sea anemones, coral and the parasitic myxozoans. Cnidarians are usually radially symmetrical, and have unique, venom-injecting stinging cells called "cnidocytes."
- **Cretaceous**- The last period of time in the Mesozoic Era, from 144 to 66 million years ago.
- **Devonian**- A period of time in the Paleozoic Era from 414 to 360 million years ago.
- **Ediacaran**- The last period of time in the Precambrian Eon from 635 to 542 million years ago.
- **Eocene**- A period of time in the Cenozoic Era from 55 to 33 million years ago.
- **Fauna**- In an ecological context, "fauna" refers to the animal components of an ecosystem.
- **Formation**- In a geological or paleontological context, a formation is a group of rock layers.
- **Gnathostome**- A gnathostome is any vertebrate chordate with a moveable jaw (or had an ancestor with one).
- **Holocene**- A period of time in the Cenozoic Era from 12,000 years ago until now.
- *Incertae sedis*- A Latin phrase literally meaning "uncertain seat." *"Incertae sedis"* is a term in classification used to refer to a species or group whose relationships with related organisms are unclear or poorly defined.
- **Jurassic**- The second period of time in the Mesozoic Era, from 199 to 145 million years ago.
- **Mesozoic**- An era of time in the Phanerozoic Eon from 249 to 66 million years ago.
- **Miocene**- A period of time in the Cenozoic Era from 23 to 5 million years ago.

- **Mollusk**- Any member of the animal phylum Mollusca, including snails, clams, squid, octopuses, tusk shells and chitons. Most mollusks have a calcium carbonate shell, and a toothed, file-like tongue called a radula. All mollusks have a cape-like organ, the mantle, which usually secretes the shell, and houses breathing organs, and a nervous system.
- **Nekton**- Any aquatic animal that lives either entirely or almost entirely in the water column, and relies on its own swimming or propulsion abilities to keep and move itself in and around the water column. Anchovies, porpoises and ichthyosaurs are examples of nekton.
- **Neogene**- The second third of the Cenozoic Era, comprising of the Miocene and the Pliocene periods.
- **Oligocene**- A period of time in the Cenozoic Era from 33 to 23 million years ago.
- **Ordovician**- A period of time in the Paleozoic Era from 484 to 440 million years ago.
- **Paleocene**- A period of time in the Cenozoic Era from 65 to 55 million years ago.
- **Paleogene**- The first third of the Cenozoic Era, comprising of the Paleocene, Eocene, and Oligocene.
- **Paleozoic**- An era of time in the Phanerozoic Eon from 249 to 66 million years ago.
- **Patagium**- Plural, "patagia." A flap-like membrane of skin used specifically by vertebrates for the purpose of gliding or flight.
- **Permian**- The last period of time in the Paleozoic Era, the time of "The Great Dying," or most severe of all known extinction events, from 299 to 250 million years ago.
- **Pharynx**- A structure in the throat of many animals located directly behind the mouth or oral chamber. In vertebrates, it often houses breathing structures, like gills.
- **Plankton**- An organism that uses water currents and waterflow to as its primary means of transportation in the water column because it is either too small to move long distances by its own power, or lacks the ability to propel itself entirely. Sargassum seaweed and jellyfish are two varieties of plankton.
- **Pleistocene**- A period of time in the Cenozoic Era from 3 million years ago until 12 thousand years ago.
- **Pliocene**- A period of time in the Cenozoic Era from 5 to 3 million years ago.
- **Quaternary**- The last third of the Cenozoic Era, comprising of the Pleistocene and the Holocene periods.
- **Terrestrial**- Living on land.
- **Triassic**- The first period of time in the Mesozoic Era, from 249 to 200 million years ago.

Name

Cattle Brand Proarticulatan

Species	*Tamga hamulifera*
Phylum	Proarticulata
Class	*incertae sedis*
Size	3 to 5mm long
Time Period	Late Ediacaran of the Precambrian, 560 million years ago
Location	The White Sea, Russia

Comments

The Cattle Brand Proarticulatan, *Tamga hamulifera*, is a tiny, freckle-sized organism that lived in a shallow sea that occupied what would eventually become the portion of Russia that, today, surrounds the White Sea.

The generic name comes from a Mongol-Turkish word meaning a "cattle brand," and refers to how the hook-like isomers form a star pattern, suggestive of a wax seal or a cattle brand. Even though the isomers form a star pattern, they also display the staggered symmetry seen in other proarticulatans, such as the Onega River proarticulatan, *Onega stepanovi*.

The form of the cattle brand proarticulatan is similar to the plates of the palaeoscolecids, a group of Early to Middle Paleozoic armored worms possibly related to the priapulids, leading some researchers to suggest that it may have been a palaeoscolecid. This hypothesis falls flat when one notices that the average body of the cattle brand proarticulatan is profoundly smaller than the average palaeoscolecid plate, and that nothing about the fossils of the cattle brand proarticulatan suggest they were mineralized like the way palaeoscolecid plates are.

Name	Clamstinet
Species	*Cambridium nikiforovae*
Phylum	?Mollusca
Class	Stenothecoida
Order	Cambridioida
Family	Cambridiidae
Size	1 to 2 centimeters in length
Time Period	"Stage 2" to "Stage 3" of the Cambrian Period, 525 to 515 million years ago
Location	Sakha Republic (Yakutia), Siberia, Russia
Comments	(Nikiforov's) Clamstinet, *Cambridium nikiforovae*, is one of several species of stenothecoids, a group of mysterious, bivalved animals that lived during the Early Cambrian. The first clamstinet fossils were originally thought to be those of monoplacophoran molluscs, a group of primitive molluscs with a bilaterally symmetrical arrangement of internal organs represented today by the deep sea *Neopilina*. Better preserved fossils showed that the first fossils of clamstinets and other stenothecoids were missing the other valves of their shells, and would have had a bodyplan unlike those of other multi-valved molluscs. While it would be easy for a layman to assume stenothecoids were like clams, the valves of stenothecoids are symmetrical, while the valves of clams are not or originally were not symmetrical. Furthermore, the articulation of stenothecoid shells differ from clams, being, instead, more similar to the unrelated brachiopods or lampshells, or, to pick a more familiar example, similar to an opened pistachio nut. Stenothecoids first arose during the Early Cambrian, and were soon ecologically displaced by the brachiopods by the Middle Cambrian.

Name	Norwegian Serpent Urchin
Species	*Volchovia norvegica*
Phylum	Echinodermata
Class	Ophiocistioidea
Family	Volchoviidae
Size	5 to 9 centimeters in diameter
Time Period	Late Arenig Epoch of the Middle Ordovician, about 467 million years ago
Location	Near Oslo, Norway
Comments	

The Norwegian Serpent Urchin, *Volchovia norvegica*, is one of a handful of peculiar echinoderms in the enigmatic class Ophiocistioidea, and are assumed to be related to sea urchins due to anatomical similarities. The class name translates as "serpent boxes," and refer to the large, and elongated tube-feet, or "podia," and how they are covered in rows of large scales, which would have made the living animals look like tiny, little boxes with snakes coming out of them. Ophiocistioids apparently had incomplete digestive tracts, as, the prominent, eye-like structure near the top of their bodies was a madreporite, a covered opening that maintains the pressure of the echinoderm water vascular system. The mouth was located on the bottom of the body, similar to the situation in sea urchins, and probably allowed the animals to graze on biofilms, or eat edible detritus.

The genus *Volchovia* is restricted to Lower Ordovician Russia, and Lower to Middle Ordovician Norway; other serpent urchins are found in Palaeozoic-aged marine strata of Eurasia, Australia and North America from the Ordovician onward, reaching their peak diversity during the Devonian, and then slowly petered out until the last serpent urchin disappears from the fossil record 254 million years ago during the Late Permian.

Name	Silurian Pirate Worm
Species	*Invavita piratica*
Phylum	Arthropoda
Subphylum	Crustacea
Class	Maxillapoda
Subclass	Pentastomida
Order	?Cephalobaenida
Size	Up to around 1.75 millimeters in length
Time Period	Wenlock epoch of the Middle Silurian, 425 million years ago
Location	England
Comments	

The Silurian Pirate Worm, *Invavita piratica*, is not the oldest pentastomid crustacean known: that honor would go to one of the Orsten Fauna pentastomids from the Late Cambrian of Öland, Sweden. The Silurian pirate worm, instead, holds the distinction of being the oldest known pentastomid whose host is clearly identified; in this case, the ostracod crustacean *Nymphatelina gravida*. Unlike most modern-day pentastomids, or "tongue worms," which are endoparasites that, as adults, live attached to the upper respiratory tracts of terrestrial vertebrates, the pirate worm lived, as an adult, attached to the shells of ostracods.

Modern-day tongue worms are, as their common name directly refers to, worm-like creatures that resemble (vertebrate) tongues; some species may or may not have leg-like podia, derived from their crustacean ancestors' legs, to help them grip the surface of their environment. Fossils, including both those of the Cambrian pentastomids, and of the pirate worm, clearly show that pentastomids achieved this body plan early in their evolutionary history, before they became endoparasites.

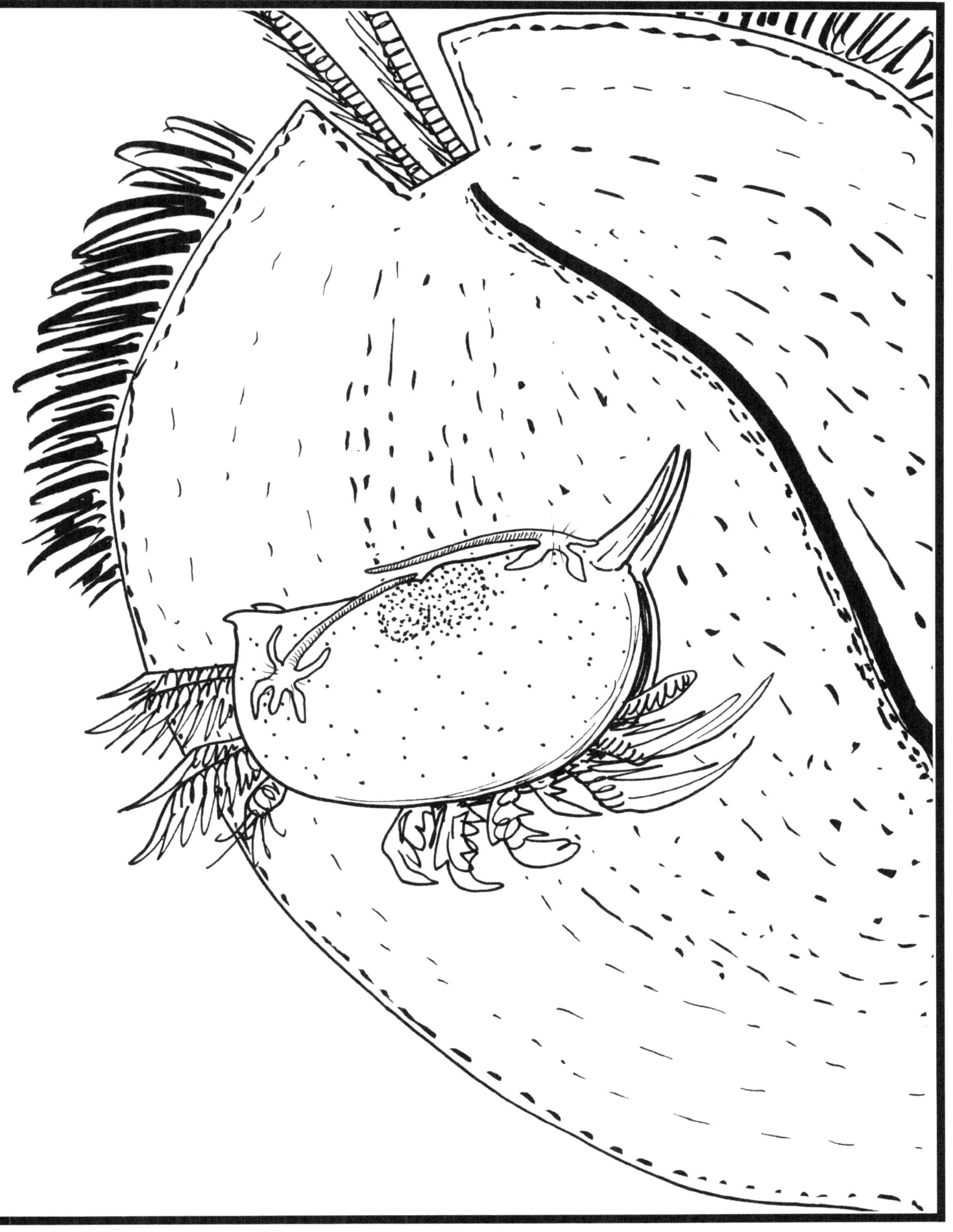

Name	Discofish
Species	*Driscollaspis pankowskiorum*
Phylum	Chordata
Class	Placodermi
Order	Arthrodira
Family	Selenosteidae
Size	Skull about 3 centimeters in length, living animal may have been up to 15 centimeters long
Time Period	Late Frasnian Epoch of the Late Devonian, 372 million years ago
Location	Nodular limestone horizon of the Kellwasser facies in Lahmida, Rheris Basin, from the Eastern Anti-Atlas Mountains, Morocco
Comments	The Discofish, *Driscollaspis pankowskiorum*, is another selenosteid arthrodire placoderm from the Late Devonian Anti-Atlas fauna in Morocco. The discofish is related to the larger Moroccan dragonfish, *Draconichthys elegans*, shown with it, who may have preyed on it. Both are endemic to Late Devonian Morocco. Like the dragonfish, the discofish is, so far, known from a single skull. The discofish lived in an algae-dimmed shallow sea that covered area in what is now Germany, and Morocco, and probably preyed on other, smaller animals

Name	Enigmammonite
Species	*Aenigmatoceras rhipaeum*
Phylum	Mollusca
Class	Cephalopoda
Subclass	Ammonoidea
Order	Goniatitida
Family	Cravenoceratidae
Size	Shell diameter about 1.3 centimeters
Time Period	Bashkirian Stage of the Early Pennsylvanian epoch of the Carboniferous, about 318 to 314 million years ago
Location	Southern Ural Mountains in Bashkortostan, Russia, and Uzbekistan
Comments	The Enigmammonite, *Aenigmatoceras rhipaeum*, is a tiny ammonite that lived on the seafloor in what is now the Ural Mountains (in the Russian federation of Bashkortostan), and in Uzbekistan.
	The enigmammonite can be identified by the three constrictions in its shell, which is superficially similar to the Carboniferous-aged ammonite *Cravenoceras*, though, whether or not the enigmammonite is related to *Cravenoceras* remains up for debate.
	The enigmammonite, like other ammonites of its size, probably fed on large foraminifera protists, a huge group of amoebae that have been producing calcium carbonate shells since the Cambrian.

Name	Spiny Elephantinite
Species	*Elephantoceras spinonodosum*
Phylum	Mollusca
Class	Cephalopoda
Subclass	Ammonoidea
Order	Goniatitida
Family	Pseudohaloritidae
Size	Shell diameter about 2 to 3 centimeters wide
Time Period	From the Roadian to the Capitanian epochs of the Middle Permian, about 268 to 265.8 million years ago
Location	Jiande, Zhejiang Provine, China
Comments	The Spiny Elephantinite, *Elephantoceras spinonodosum*, is a member of one of several Permian-aged ammonite lineages from China. Ammonites of the genus *Elephantoceras* are named so for the fact that in intact shells, the shell-mouth has upward-curving lappets or flaps that reminded the original describers of elephant's tusks. The spines on the spiny elephantinite's shell (and the nodules on the shell of the related nodular elephantinite, *E. nodosum*) hinder the animal's hydrodynamic ability, so that these, coupled with the broad keel of the shell meant that the elephantinites were not speedy swimmers. Most likely, they, like the Enigmammonite, were slow swimmers, or possibly even benthic crawlers who preyed on foraminifera.

Name	(Aleksander Grigorevich) Sharov's Flyer
Species	*Sharovipteryx mirabilis*
Phylum	Chordata
Class	Reptilia
Order	Protorosauria
Family	Sharovipterygidae
Size	"Wing"span estimated to be about 30 centimeters
Time Period	Late Triassic, about 225 million years ago
Location	Madygen Formation in the Fergana Valley, Kyrgyzstan
Comments	Even by prehistoric standards, the (Aleksander Grigorevich) Sharov's Flyer, *Sharovipteryx mirabilis*, was a profoundly peculiar animal. In contrast to almost all other known gliding vertebrates, Sharov's flyer apparently glided by using primarily the patagia stretched across the hindlegs. If the forelegs had patagia stretched across them, too, then the Sharov's flyer would have been able to glide like a delta-wing aircraft, in that, the animal would have been able to control its aerial maneuverabilty and steering by manipulating the angle it held its forelegs at. Unfortunately, too much of the matrix of the holotype, and only known specimen, was cleared away during preparation, and any trace of the foreleg patagia, if any, was destroyed. Sharov's flyer is a protorosaurian, a member of a group of primitive reptiles closely related to choristoderans, turtles and archosaurs (i.e., crocodilians, dinosaurs and pterosaurs).

Name	False Nautilus
Species	*Pseudonautilus geinitzi*
Phylum	Mollusca
Class	Cephalopoda
Order	Nautilida
Family	Pseudonautilidae
Size	Shell diameter from 2 to 3 centimeters
Time Period	Tithonian Epoch of the Late Jurassic Period, 152 to 145 million years ago
Location	Stramberger Formation from Stramberg, Moravia (in the Czech Republic)
Comments	The False Nautiluses of the family Pseudonautilidae superficially resemble, shell-wise, their still-living relatives, the "true" nautiluses of Nautilidae, and probably occupied similar ecological niches as predators of crustaceans, though, true nautiluses tend to grow much larger than the false nautiluses. Each family represents a different branch of the superfamily Nautilaceae.
	The internal architecture of the shells of the false nautiluses of the genus *Pseudonautilus*, however, closely resemble that of the Permian-aged nautilids of the genus *Permoceras*.
	Shown here is Geinitz's False Nautilus, *Pseudonautilus geinitzi*, of Late Jurassic Stramberg, Moravia. Related species are found in similar-aged marine strata of Ukraine, and earliest Cretaceous-aged marine strata of Tunisia.

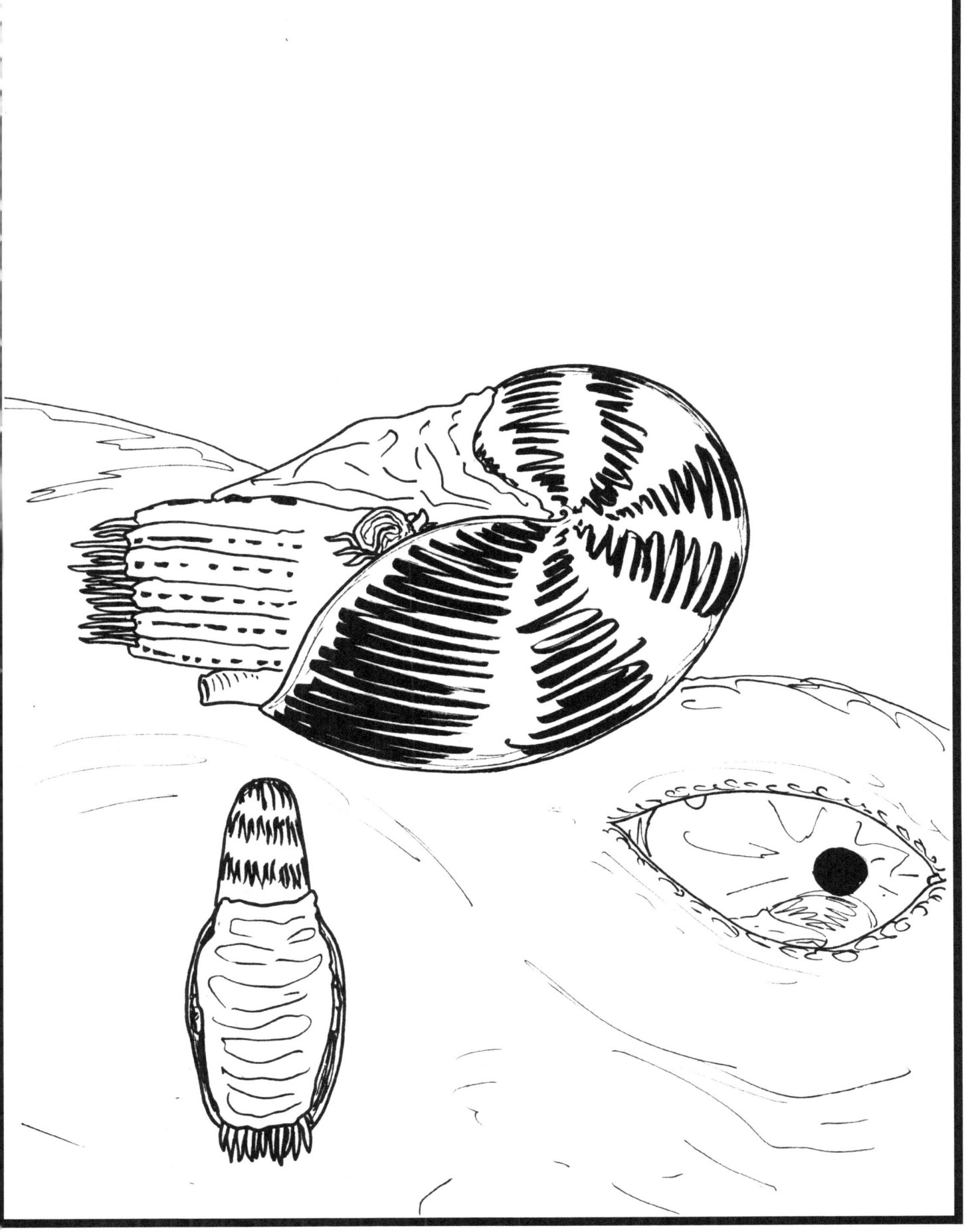

Name	Voracious Possumodon
Species	*Didelphodon vorax*
Phylum	Chordata
Class	Mammalia
clade	Metatheria
clade	Marsupialiformes
Family	Stagodontidae
Size	Slightly larger than a modern-day Virginia oppossum, may have weighed around 5 kilograms
Time Period	Campanian to Maastrichtian epoches of the Late Cretaceous, from 77 to 66 million years ago
Location	Hell Creek Formation, Montana and North Dakota
Comments	The Voracious Possumodon, *Didelphodon vorax*, is the largest known mammal of Late Cretaceous North America, about the size of a Virgina oppossum, , and surpassed only in size by the Early Cretaceous triconodont, *Repenomanus giganticus*, which is about the size of a large housecat.

Almost complete skulls and intact teeth suggest the animal was carnivorous, and ate hard materials, such as bone or molluscs. But because the skulls are not highly vaulted like those of mammals that specialize in eating bones, like hyenas, the voracious and other possumodons probably ate other, softer foods, too, such as insects, carrion and small vertebrates. The bone structure of the paws suggest either webbed feet similar to the paws of otters, or fairly rigid feet. Proponents of the former suggest that some, if not all species of possumodons were semiaquatic, like otters, and point to a fossil of an unidentified species found in a riverbed as further proof.

The voracious possumodon is found in the Hell Creek Formation in Montana and North Dakota: related species are found in similar-aged formations nearby in Wyoming and Canada.

Name	Dragon Mesonychid
Species	*Ankalagon saurognathus*
Phylum	Chordata
Class	Mammalia
Order	Mesonychia
Family	Mesonychidae
Size	Male estimated to be about the size of a black bear: female possibly the size of a timber wolf.
Time Period	Torrejonian epoch of the Paleocene, 63.3 to 60 million years ago
Location	San Juan Basin, New Mexico, United States
Comments	The Dragon Mesonychid, *Ankalagon saurognathus*, is one of the largest mesonychids in North America, living what is now New Mexico during the Early Paleocene. The dragon mesonychid is descended from the wide-ranging genus *Dissacus*, which originated in Mongolia, and, by the Middle Paleocene, spread into Europe, as well as North America.

The dragon mesonychid was originally described as a very large species of *Dissacus* (species of which otherwise grew to the size of small dogs or jackals), based off of a mandible that belonged to an animal the size of a black bear. Because of this profound size difference, '*Dissacus*' *saurognathus* was placed into its own genus, *Ankalagon*. The name is a direct reference to a dragon, "Ancalagon the Black," in the book <u>Silmarillion</u>: the researchers would have used the original spelling, but, that was already taken for a Cambrian worm. Additional, similar mandibles were found, eventually leading researchers to realize that the dragon mesonychid was sexually dimorphic, in that the males were bear-sized and heavily built, while the females were timber wolf-sized, and more graceful in comparison. It may be that the two genders also occupied different ecological roles, as well, with the males scavenging carrion and eating bones, while the females hunted small prey.

Name	Wolf Mesonychid
Species	*Mesonyx obtusidens*
Phylum	Chordata
Class	Mammalia
Order	Mesonychia
Family	Mesonychidae
Size	Similar in size to a timber wolf.
Time Period	Bridgerian Epoch of the Middle Eocene, 49.5 to 46 million years ago
Location	Bridger Formation, Wyoming, similar-aged formations in Utah and Colorado.
Comments	The Wolf Mesonychid, *Mesonyx obtusidens*, is the earliest described, and one of the best known mesonychids. The name "Mesonyx" translates as "middle/intermediate claw," in reference to how the beast was originally though to be an evolutionary intermediary between the Creodonts and the Carnivorans. Later, the teeth of *M. obtusidens* and other mesonychids, especially their large, flattened multipronged, multicusped molars, were very similar to those of primitive whales. This extreme similarity lead to a longlived theory that whales evolved from mesonychians, with both groups being closely related to cloven-hoofed, or artiodactyl mammals. The discovery of primitive artiodactyls with whale-like bullae, and the discovery of primitive whales with the "pulley" astragulus or wristbone diagnostic of artiodactyls, and noting that mesonychians lack both features, put a stake through that theory.

Now, mesonychians are thought to be primitive ungulates related to both artiodactyls and odd-toed, or perissodactyl mammals (horses, rhinoceri, etc), while whales are (descendants of) artiodactyls closely related to hippopotami.

The wolf mesonychid lived in what is now the states of Wyoming, Utah, and Colorado during the Middle Eocene, its ancestors having emigrated into North America from China and Mongolia during the Early Eocene. It was a bone-crunching, wolf-sized, tropical forest-dwelling predator that probably also scavenged carcasses.

Name	Bandit Mesonychid
Species	*Mongolestes hadrodens*
Phylum	Chordata
Class	Mammalia
Order	Mesonychia
Family	Mesonychidae
Size	Probably about the size of a large dog
Time Period	Ulangochuian to Rupellian Epochs of the Late Eocene to Early Oligocene, from 37 to 34 million years ago
Location	"Ulan Gochu" of the Baron Sog Mesa, Inner Mongolia, China
Comments	The Bandit Mesonychid, *Mongolestes hadrodens*, is the last known mesonychid and mesonychian, its fossils being found in Inner Mongolia, China.

The Bandit Mesonychid, *Mongolestes hadrodens*, is the last known mesonychid and mesonychian, its fossils being found in Inner Mongolia, China.

During the Early Paleogene, from the Paleocene to Eocene, mesonychians were important predatory mammals in Chinese and North American ecosystems. During the Eocene, mesonychians faced stiff competition from the hyaenodonts, and from primitive carnivorans, and were eventually ecologically displaced by both groups until only the bandit mesonychid remained.

The bandit mesonychid differs from other mesonychids in having comparatively larger teeth, and no third molar. The bandit mesonychid has a very steep mandibular symphysis, suggesting a very powerful bite.

Name	(G. H. R. von Koenigswald's) Gargano Moonrat
Species	*Deinogalerix koenigswaldi*
Phylum	Chordata
Class	Mammalia
Order	Eulipotyphla
Family	Erinaceidae
Size	Skull up to 20 centimeters
Time Period	Tortonian Epoch of the Late Miocene, 10 to 8 million years ago
Location	Farm of San Giovannino, Gargano, Italy
Comments	The Gargano Moonrats of the genus *Deinogalerix* are the largest members of the hedgehog family, Erinaceidae, though the Gargano moonrats are more closely related to the moonrats, or gymnures, of *Echinosorex*, which lack spines and look more like a rat or possum.

The (G. H. R. von Koenigswald's) Gargano Moonrat, *D. koenigswaldi*, is the youngest, and largest of this group of housecat-sized moonrats. During the Middle to Late Miocene, the peninsula was a forested, volcanic island in an archipelago. It is hypothesized that moonrats of the extinct genus *Parasorex* came to the island near the end of the Middle Miocene, and evolved into the first species, the least Gargano moonrat, *D. minor*, which is known from teeth. The Koenigswald's Gargano moonrat coexists with the shortsnouted Gargano moonrat, *D. brevirostirs*: some researchers speculate that the two species actually represent sexual dimorphism.

The Gargano moonrats, the Koenigswald's in particular, are thought to have evolved their enormous sizes in order to better prey on a diverse fauna of endemic rodents and terrestrial invertebrates. The Gargano moonrats, themselves, were probably preyed on by several of the endemic birds of prey, including the giant barn owls *Tyto robusta* and *T. gigantea*, and species of the extinct eagle genus *Garganoaetus*.

Name   Borson's Mastodon

Species   *Zygolophodon borsoni*

Phylum   Chordata

Class   Mammalia

Order   Proboscidea

Family   Mammutidae

Size   About 3.5 meters at the shoulder

Time Period Latest Miocene to Late Pliocene, from 6 to 2.5 million years ago

Location   Europe

Comments   Borson's Mastodon, *Zygolophodon borsoni*, is a very large European species of a wide-ranging genus of mastodon proboscidean with other species in Africa, Asia and North America. Mastodons superficially resemble their relatives, the true elephants of Elephantidae, but differ in terms of skull and tooth anatomies.

Borson's mastodon would have resembled a large elephant, but with a subtly elongated head, and a pair of enormously elongated tusks over three meters long. And, should it open its mouth, an observer might also notice a second pair of very small tusks in its lower jaw. This mastodon first appeared in Europe near the end of the Miocene, probably entering in from Northern Africa, and spread northward. The Borson's mastodon also competed with elephants that began appearing during the Late Pliocene, and were eventually driven into extinction by this competition.

Name

(South) American Giant Ground Sloth

Species	*Megatherium americanum*
Phylum	Chordata
Class	Mammalia
Superorder	Xenarthra
Order	Pilosa
Family	Megatheriidae
Size	About 2.1 meters at the shoulders, 6 meters from head to tail.
Time Period	Early Pliocene to Early Holocene, from 4 million to 10 thousand years ago.
Location	South America.
Comments	The (South) American Giant Ground Sloth, *Megatherium americanum*, is one of the very first prehistoric animals officially described, the first bones excavated in 1788, in Argentina. *M. americanum* is also the largest known xenarthran, and is one of the largest terrestrial mammals known, surpassed in size by some mammoths and the giant rhinoceros, *Paraceratherium*.

The American giant ground sloth is known from numerous fossils, from eroded bones to dried hair and dung, found throughout South America: fossils of the similar, more northerly ranging *Eremotherium* have lead people to mistakenly believe the genus *Megatherium* ranged into North America.

The American giant ground sloth lived in open grasslands, woodlands and arid scrub, and fed on tough vegetation. Using its stout tail as extra support, the giant ground sloth could stand up on its hindlegs to assume a bipedal/tripedal stance, probably to tear leaves and branches out of trees. Its great size meant that the adults were ignored by the local predatory animals.

Name	# Fiji Giant Iguana
Species	*Lapitiguana impensa*
Phylum	Chordata
Class	Reptilia
Order	Squamata
Suborder	Sauria
Family	Iguanidae
Size	Possibly similar in size to, or slightly larger than a rhinoceros iguana, genus *Cyclura*.
Time Period	Holocene: Became extinct around 1000 BCE, when Fiji was first colonized by the Lapita People
Location	Fiji Islands, in the Pacific Ocean
Comments	The Fiji Giant Iguana, *Lapitiguana impensa*, is a very large, extinct iguana endemic to the islands of Fiji, and is thought to be closely related to the living Fiji iguanas of genus *Brachylophus*.

The Fiji Giant Iguana, *Lapitiguana impensa*, is a very large, extinct iguana endemic to the islands of Fiji, and is thought to be closely related to the living Fiji iguanas of genus *Brachylophus*.

In life, the Fiji giant iguana is thought to have been very much like most large iguanian lizards, being strict, somewhat sluggish, diurnal herbivores that ate almost exclusively leaves, fruit, and the occasional flower. The generic name refers to the Lapita People, a race of pottery-making seafarers who settled in Fiji around 3 thousand years ago, and whose appearance uncoincidentally coincides with the giant iguana's extinction. In the picture are a pair of the extinct Viti Levu pigeon, *Natunaornis gigoura*.

The presence of iguanids, who are otherwise restricted to the New World, in Polynesia seemingly defies explanation. A hypothesis was once made, when the Madagascar iguanas of genera *Oplura* and *Chalarodon* were still considered to be within Iguanidae, that the Fiji iguanas represent the final redoubt of an Old World iguana lineage that island-hopped to Polynesia via Southeast Asia and or Australia. Now that the Madagascar iguanas have been determined, through mitochondrial DNA tests, to have split from the true iguanas of Iguanidae during the Jurassic, and that no true (or non Oplurid) iguanas are known in the Old World younger than the youngest species of *Arretosaurus* of Early Oligocene Mongolia, coupled with the fact that the Fiji iguanas are more closely related to New World iguanas, it's now assumed that the Fiji iguanas probably rafted over from South America.

Bibliography

- Aksarina, N. A., and Yu S. Nadler. "New Stenothecoida species from the Lower Cambrian of Kuznetsk Alatau (Kiya reference section)." *RUSSIAN GEOLOGY AND GEOPHYSICS C/C OF GEOLOGIIA I GEOFIZIKA* 40.7 (1999): 1017-1027.
- Butler, Percy Milton. *The giant erinaceid insectivore, Deinogalerix Freudenthal, from the upper Miocene of Gargano, Italy.* Rijksmuseum van Geologie en Mineralogie, 1980.
- Dzik, Jerzy, and Tomasz Sulej. "An early Late Triassic long-necked reptile with a bony pectoral shield and gracile appendages." *Acta Palaeontologica Polonica* 61.4 (2016): 805-823.
- Van der Geer, Alexandra, et al. *Evolution of island mammals: adaptation and extinction of placental mammals on islands.* John Wiley & Sons, 2011.
- van Diggelen, J. "Overzicht van de Mesozoische en Cenozoische Nautiloidea." *GEA* 27.2 (1994): 45-51.
- Fox, R.C.; Naylor, B.G. (2006). "Stagodontid marsupials from the Late Cretaceous of Canada and their systematic and functional implications" (PDF). Acta Palaeontologica Polonica. 51 (6): 13–36.
- Freudenthal, Matthijs. *Deinogalerix koenigswaldi nov. gen., nov. spec., a giant insectivore from the Neogene of Italy.* Rijksmuseum van Geologie en Mineralogie, 1972.
- Gans, Carl; Darevski, Ilya; Tatarinov, Leonid P. (1987). "*Sharovipteryx,* a reptilian glider?". *Paleobiology.* **13** (4): 415–426
- Ivantsov, A. Yu. "Small Vendian transversely articulated fossils." *Paleontological Journal* 41.2 (2007): 113-122.
- Jin, Xun. "Mesonychids from Lushi Basin, Henan Province, China." *Vertebrata Pal Asiatica* 43.2 (2004): 151-164.
- Lund, Richard. "Photomacrography of fossils for publication." *Journal of Paleontology* (1980): 264-266.
- O'LEARY, MAUREEN A., Spencer G. Lucas, and Thomas E. Williamson. "A new specimen of Ankalagon (Mammalia, Mesonychia) and evidence of sexual dimorphism in mesonychians." *Journal of Vertebrate Paleontology* 20.2 (2000): 387-393.
- Pregill, Gregory K., and Trevor H. Worthy. "A new iguanid lizard (Squamata, Iguanidae) from the late Quaternary of Fiji, Southwest Pacific." *Herpetologica* 59.1 (2003): 57-67.
- Regnell, Gerhard. "Echinoderms (Hydrophoridea, Ophiocistia) from the Ordovician (Upper Skiddavian, 3c) of the Oslo Region." *NORSK GEOL TIDSSKR* 27 (1948): 14-58.
- Reich, M., and R. Haude. "Ophiocistioidea (fossil Echinodermata): an overview." *Echinoderms: München. Taylor & Francis, London* (2004): 489-494.
- Rücklin, Martin, John A. Long, and Kate Trinajstic. "A new selenosteid arthrodire ('Placodermi') from the Late Devonian of Morocco." *Journal of Vertebrate Paleontology* 35.2 (2015): e908896.
- V. E. Ruzhentsev and M. F. Bogoslovskaya. 1978. Namyurskii etap v evolyutsii ammonoidyey - Namurian stage, evolution of ammonoids. *Trudyi*

paleontologicheskovo instituta **167**:1-338

- Siveter, David J., et al. "A 425-million-year-old Silurian pentastomid parasitic on ostracods." *Current Biology* 25.12 (2015): 1632-1637.
- Szalay, Frederick S., and Stephen Jay Gould. "Asiatic Mesonychidae (Mammalia, Condylarthra). Bulletin of the AMNH; v. 132, article 2." (1966).
- Turner, Alan. *National Geographic Prehistoric Mammals*. National Geographic, 2004.
- Van Valen, Leigh. "Ankalagon, new name (Mammalia; Condylartha)." *Journal of Paleontology* 54.1 (1980): 266.
- Villier, Boris, et al. "New discoveries on the giant hedgehog Deinogalerix from the Miocene of Gargano (Apulia, Italy)." *Geobios* 46.1 (2013): 63-75.
- Wilson, G.P.; Ekdale, E.G.; Hoganson, J.W.; Calede, J.J.; Linden, A.V. (2016). "A large carnivorous mammal from the Late Cretaceous and the North American origin of marsupials". Nature Communications. 7.
- Yochelson, Ellis L. "StenothecoidaStenothecoida." *Paleontology*. Springer Berlin Heidelberg, 1979. 767-768.
- Zhao Jinke, and Zheng Zhaogong. "Late Triassic in the West of Zhejiang and Jiangxi," Paleontology 16.2 (1977): 217-252. (赵金科, and 郑灼官. "浙西, 赣东北早二叠世晚期菊石." 古生物学报 16.2 (1977): 217-252.)

About the Artist

Stanton F. Fink is a student of Biology and Chinese Medicine, and makes a hobby of drawing monsters and researching flowers, arcane-looking creatures, prehistoric animals, fish, reptiles, birds and the occasional, really grotesque fungal fruiting body.

Stanton grew up and went to school in California and is currently living, drawing, and gardening in Oregon.

www.ingramcontent.com/pod-product-compliance
Lightning Source LLC
Chambersburg PA
CBHW081125280526

45787CB00007B/2990